The
Healing
Of A
Man .

Mark 2 : 1 - 12

By

John C Burt.

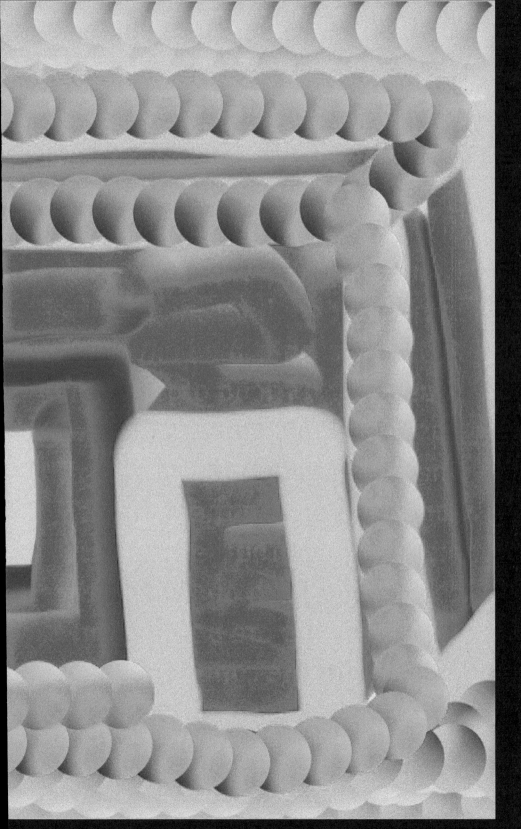

FOREWORD :

Mark 2 : 1 - 12; ' The Healing of A Man ', is an important book for me to write? At this present time I am in a season for a friend of mine who has cancer, his name is Richard. These verses and the story contained within them, helps me to believe that Jesus Christ can see my faith and the faith of others who are praying my friend with the cancer?

A lot of times we can blame the person who is not healed for their own lack of faith? In Mark 2 : 1 - 12 Jesus Christ is not so much concerned with the faith of the paralyzed man as he is concerned with the faith of the four men who bring the man to Him? I find this helpful as I and you seek to engage in praying for our friends who are in need of a healing touch from Jesus Christ?

Even with a little faith lots of things in and through

Jesus Christ. Think about the ' faith of a mustard seed ' and how Jesus Christ said that size of faith was enough to achieve much for Him and His Kingdom. Sometimes and I guess if you are like me, most of the time, we / I believe we need to have mountains of real faith in prayer for the outcome we desire to happen for the person we are praying for. Its so easy to forget that even a little faith can be used by Jesus Christ to produce much effect and results? Believing even a little bit can and does have great impact;

the Son, the Father and the Holy Spirit can use and energize things on the basis of that faith.

I always think; particularly after reading Mark 2 : 1 - 12 that faith is the currency of the realm, in the Kingdom of God, the Kingdom of the beloved Son Jesus Christ? It may well be the plain truth that we do not always have enough faith ourselves to believe that Jesus Christ can heal the person we are praying for?

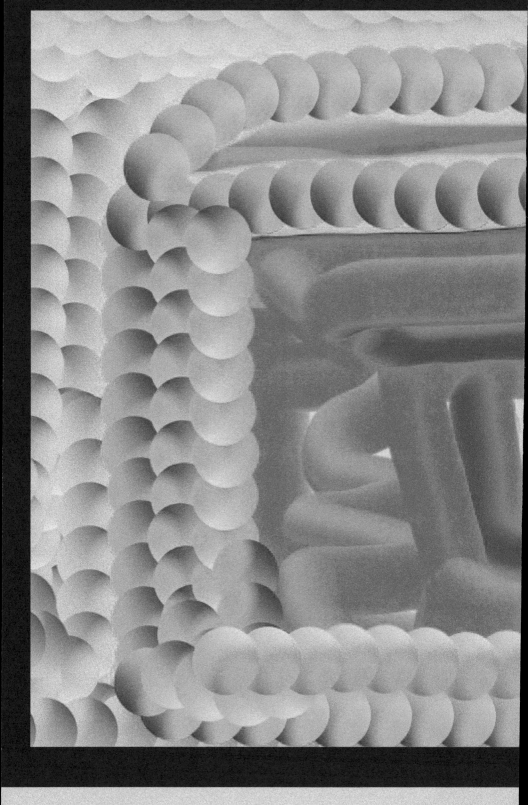

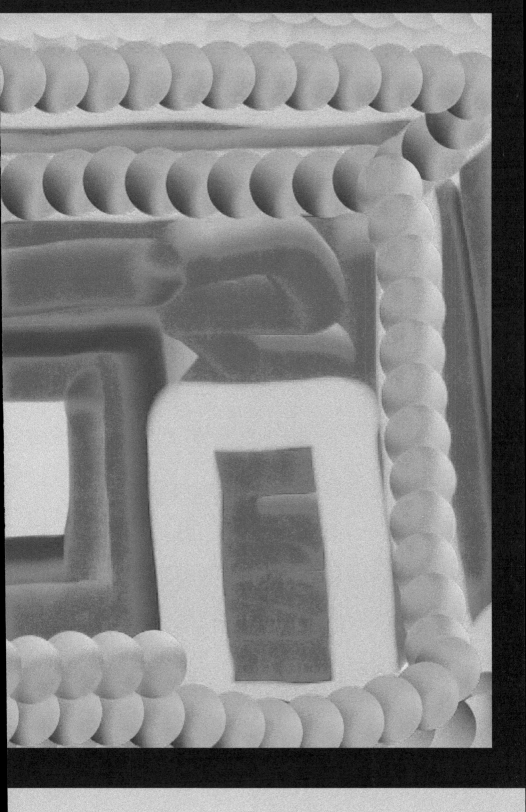

Mark 2 : 1 - 12

{ CEB }

(1) " After a few days, Jesus went back to Caperrnaum, and people heard that he was at home.

(2) So many gathered that there was no longer space, not even near the door. Jesus was speaking the word to them.

(3) Some people arrived, and four of them were bringing to him a man who was paralyzed.

(4) They couldn't carry him through the crowd, so they tore off part of the roof above where Jesus was . When they had made an opening, they lowered the mat on which the paralyzed man was lying.

(5) When Jesus saw their

faith, he said to the paralytic, " Child, your sins are forgiven!"

(6) Some legal experts were sitting there, muttering among themselves,

(7) " Why does he speak this way? He's insulting God. Only the one God can forgive sins."

(8) Jesus immediately recognized what they were discussing, and he said to them,

" Why do you fill your minds with these questions?

(9) Which is easier - to say to a paralyzed person, ' Your sins are forgiven', or to say ' Get up, take up your bed, and walk'?

(10) But so you will know that the Human One has authority on the earth to forgive sins" - he said to the man who was paralyzed,

(11) " Get up, take your mat, and go home."

(12) Jesus raised him up, and right away he picked up his mat and walked out in front of everybody. They were all amazed and praised God, saying, " We've never seen anything like this."

Mark 2 : 1 - 12

{ Heb - Gk Study Bible NIV }

(1) " A few days later, when Jesus again entered Caperrnaum, the people heard that he had come home.

(2) So many gathered that there was no room left, not even outside the door, and he preached the word to them.

(3) Some men came, bringing to him a paralytic, carried by four of them.

(4) Since they could not get him to Jesus because of the crowd, they made an opening in the roof above Jesus and, after digging through it, lowered the mat the paralyzed man was lying on.

(5) When Jesus saw their faith, he said to the paralytic, " Son, your sins are forgiven."

(6) Now some teachers of the Law were sitting there,

thinking to themselves,

(7) " Why does this fellow talk like that? He's blaspheming! Who can forgive sins but God alone?"

(8) Immediately Jesus knew in his spirit that this was what they were thinking in their hearts, and he said to them, " Why are you thinking these things?

(9) Which is easier: to say to the paralytic, " Your sins are forgiven", or to say, " Get up, take your mat and walk?"

(10) But that you may know that the Son of Man has authority on earth to forgive sins ...... " He said to the paralytic,

(11) " I tell you, get up, take your mat and go home."

(12) He got up, took his mat

and walked out in full view of them all. This amazed everyone and they praised God, saying, " We have never seen anything like this!"

Mark 2 : 1 - 12

{ ESV }

(1) " And when he returned to Caperrnaum after some days, it was reported that he was at home.

(2) And many were gathered together, so that there was no more room, not even at the door. And he was preaching the word to them.

(3) And they came, bringing to him a paralytic carried by four men.

(4) And when they could not get near him because of the crowd, they removed the roof above him, and when they had

made an opening , they let down the bed on which the paralytic lay.

(5) And when Jesus saw their faith, he said to the paralytic, " Son, your sins are forgiven."

(6) Now some of the scribes were sitting there, questioning in their hearts.

(7) " Why does this man speak like that? He is blaspheming!

Who can forgive sins but God alone?"

(8) And immediately Jesus, perceiving in his spirit that they thus questioned within themselves, said to them ,
" Why do you question these things in your hearts?

(9) Which is easier, to say to the paralytic, ' Your sins are forgiven', or to say, ' Rise, take up your bed and walk?'

(10) But that you may
know that the Son of Man has
authority on earth to forgive
sins' - he said to the paralytic-

(11) " I say to you, rise,
pick up your bed, and go
home."

(12) And he rose and
immediately picked up his
bed and went out before
them all, so that they were all
amazed and glorified God,

saying , " We never saw anything like this ! "

Mark 2 : 1 - 12

{ GNT }

(1) " A few days later Jesus went back to Caperrnaum, and the news spread that he was at home.

(2) So many people came together that there was no

room left, not even out in front of the door. Jesus was preaching the message to them.

(3) When four men arrived, carrying a paralyzed man to Jesus.

(4) Because of the crowd, however, they could not get the man to him. So they made a hole in the roof right above the place where Jesus was. When they had

made an opening, they let the man down, lying on his mat.

(5) Seeing how much faith they had, Jesus said to the paralyzed man, " My son, your sins are forgiven."

(6) Some teachers of the Law who were sitting there thought to themselves,

(7) " How does he dare to talk like this ? This is blasphemy!

God is the only one who can forgive sins! "

(8) At once Jesus knew what they were thinking, so he said to them, " Why do you think such things?"

(9) Is it easier to say to this paralyzed man, ' Your sins are forgiven,' or to say , ' Get up, pick up your mat, and walk?'

(10) I will prove to you, then, that the Son of Man has authority on earth to forgive sins'. So he said to the paralyzed man,

(11) ' I tell you, pick up your mat, and go home.'

(12) While they all watched, the man got up, picked up his mat, and hurried away. They were all amazed and praised God, saying, " We have never seen

anything like this."

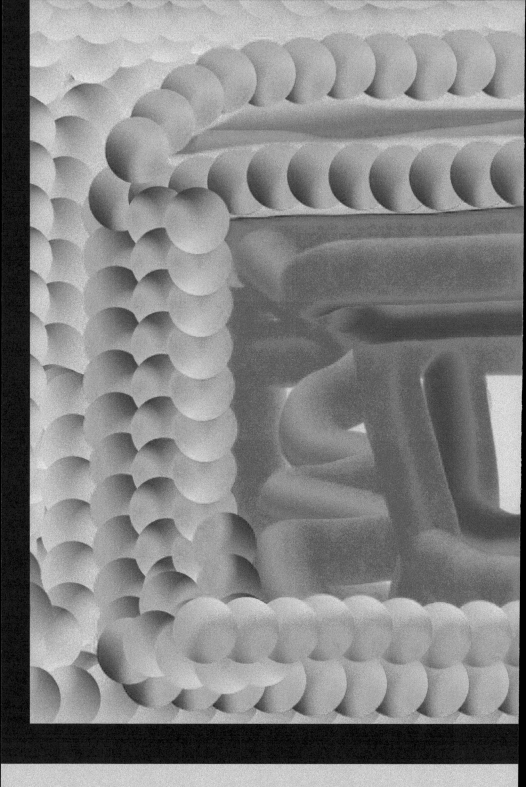

What I would like to do now, is to give you at least two different versions of the story from Mark 2: 1 - 12 in two other gospels. That is from Matthew 9 : 1 - 8 and Luke 5 : 17 - 26 .

Matthew 9 : 1 - 8

{ CEB}

(1) " Boarding a boat, Jesus crossed to the other side of the

lake and went to his own
city.

(2) People brought to him a
man who was paralyzed,
lying on a cot. When Jesus
saw their faith, he said to the
man who was paralyzed, "
Be encouraged , my child,
your sins are forgiven."

(3) Some legal experts said
among themselves, " This

man is insulting God."

(4) But Jesus knew what they were thinking and said, " Why do you fill your minds with evil things?

(5) Which is easier - to say, ' Your sins are forgiven,' or to say, ' Get up and walk?'

(6) But so you will know that the Human One has authority on the earth to forgive sins" -

he said to the man who was paralyzed - " Get up, take up your cot, and go home."

(7) The man got up and went home.

(8) When the crowds saw what had happened, they were afraid and praised God, who had given such authority to human beings."

Luke 5 : 17 - 26

{ CEB }

(17) " One day when Jesus was teaching, Pharisees and legal experts were sitting nearby. They had come from every village in Galilee and Judea, and from Jerusalem. Now the power of the Lord was with Jesus to heal.

(18) Some men were bringing

a man who was paralyzed, lying on a cot. They wanted to carry him in and place him before Jesus,

(19) both they couldn't reach him because of the crowd. So they took him up on the roof and lowered him - cot and all - through the roof tiles into the crowded room in front of Jesus.

(20) When Jesus saw their

faith, he said, " Friend, your sins are forgiven."

(21) The legal experts and Pharisees began to mutter amongst themselves, " Who is this who insults God? Only God can forgive sins!"

(22) Jesus recognized what they were discussing and responded, " Why do you fill your minds with these questions?

(23) Which is easier - to say,

' Your sins are forgiven, ' or to say , ' Get up and walk'?

(24) But so that you will know that the Human One has authority on the earth to forgive sins" - Jesus now spoke to the man who was paralyzed, " I say to you, get up, take your cot, and go home."

(25) Right away, the man stood before them, picked up

his cot, and went home, praising God.

(26) All the people were beside themselves with wonder. Filled with awe, they glorified God, saying, " We've seen unimaginable things today."

Matthew 9 : 1 - 8

{ Heb - Gk Study Bible NIV }

(1) " Jesus stepped into a boat,

crossed over and came to his own town.

(2) Some men brought to him a paralytic, lying on a mat. When Jesus saw their faith, he said to the paralytic, " Take heart, son; your sins are forgiven."

(3) At this, some of the teachers of the law said to themselves, " This fellow is blaspheming! "

(4) Knowing their thoughts, Jesus said, " Why do you entertain evil thoughts in your hearts?

(5) Which is easier : to say, ' Your sins are forgiven, ' or to say, ' Get up and walk'?

(6) But so that you may know that the Son of Man has authority on earth to forgive sins...." Then he said to the paralytic, " Get up, take your

mat and go home."

(7) And the man got up and went home.

(8) When the crowd saw this, they were filled with awe; and they praised Go, who had given such authority to men."

Luke 5 : 17 - 26

{ Heb - Gk Study Bible NIV }

(17) One day as he was teaching, Pharisees and teachers of the law, who had come from every village of Galilee and from Judea and Jerusalem, were sitting there. And the power of the Lord was present for him to heal the sick.

(18) Some men came carrying a paralytic on a mat and tried to take him into the house to lay him before Jesus.

(19) When they could not find a way to do this because of the crowd, they went up on the roof and lowered him on his mat through the tiles into the middle of the crowd, right in front of Jesus.

(20) When Jesus saw their faith, he said, " Friend, your sins are forgiven."

(21) The Pharisees and the

teachers of the law began thinking to themselves, " Who is this fellow who speaks blasphemy? Who can forgive sins but God alone?"

(22) Jesus knew what they were thinking and asked, " Why are you thinking these things in your hearts?

(23) Which is easier: to say, ' Your sins are forgiven,' or to say, " Get up and walk'?

(24) But that you may know that the Son of Man has authority on earth to forgive sins....." He said to the paralyzed man, " I tell you, get up, take your mat and go home."

(25) Immediately he stood up in front of them, took what he had been lying on and went home praising God.

(26) Everyone was amazed

and gave praise to God. They were filled with awe and said, " We have seen remarkable things today."

1. Verses One and two : - The crowds gather to hear from Jesus Christ.

Mark 2 : 1 - 2

{ Heb - Gk Study Bible NIV }

(1) " A few days later, when Jesus again entered Caperrnaum, the people heard that he had come home.

(2) So many gathered that there was no room left, not even outside the door, and he preached the word to them."

Mark 2 : 1 - 2

{ ESV }

(1) " And when he returned to Caperrnaum after some days, it was reported that he was at home.

(2) And many were gathered together, so that there was no more room, not even at the door. And he was preaching the word to them."

Mark 2 : 1 - 2

{ GNT }

(1) " A few days later Jesus went back to Caperrnaum, and the news spread that he was at home.

(2) So many people came together that there was no room left, not even in front of the door. Jesus was preaching the message to them."

Mark 2 : 1 - 2

{ CEB }

(1) " After a few days, Jesus went back to Caperrnaum, and people heard that he was at home.

(2) So many gathered that there was no longer space, not even near the door. Jesus was speaking the word to them."

Verse one begins with an update on the movements of Jesus Christ. The news spread that he had come back into the town of Caperrnaum, ' What was he going to do now?' In many ways the scene pictured in verse one is like many communities in Africa, the Middle East and even Asia, when a person arrives in a community again for a visit, everybody in that particular community soon knows that person is again in their community? I sometimes think of it being like ' the coconut wireless ' ; it is a means of broadcasting the community news without a wireless?

Its interesting to think through what the words ' at home ' mean, was it the home of Jesus Christ or the home of one of His disciple's in Caperrnaum? We are taught basically that Jesus Christ was in reality
' homeless ' ; He had no home of His own? The importance of this lies in the fact that if Jesus Christ was ' homeless ' , He could be more identified with the disadvantaged and marginalized of today?

Verse two paints a word picture for us of a home with a massive crowd in it and around it? People were wanting to see Jesus Christ up close and personal in Caperrnaum, or so it seems? Whether or not this was the rent - a - crowd of the later scenes of Palm Sunday in the City of Jerusalem is debatable? This crowd at Caperrnaum was different, they had heard and some may have even seen what Jesus Christ had done in other parts of this area? They now

Its like in our day of celebrities who write books and star in movies , the ultimate book tour?

The crowds were that massive that all parts of the house that they were meeting in were filled up. Even the space around the door in and out and around the space of it was filled up with people. This word picture can still be found in reality in Africa, the Middle East and parts of Asia. When somebody comes to town, everybody wants to see them and they may well crowd around and in the person's home the person is staying in? In the West the crowd scene in and around the house may seem to be an unusual event, yet in many parts of the majority world it would not be that unusual for there to be such a crowd around a house?

The ' word ' preached by Jesus Christ

to the crowds is an interesting thing to think through? Usually one would think of Jesus Christ preaching ' words ' to the crowds around Him at any given time. It may hint at the fact that Jesus Christ preached from the Scriptures of the Old Testament, their Scriptures at that time. Its interesting to speculate on what passage He would have been speaking to and from? Yet, to be honest we are just not told in these verses from Mark's gospel? One wonders even further if it were a ' word ' for the people crowded around and in that house in Caperrnaum at that period of time?

2. Verses Three and Four : - the paralytic arrives, carried by four men to Jesus Christ.

Mark 2 : 3 - 4

{ CEB }

(3) " Some people arrived, and four of them were bringing to him a man who was paralyzed.

(4) They couldn't carry him through the crowd, so they tore off part of the roof above where Jesus was. When they had made an opening, they lowered the mat on which the paralyzed man was lying."

Mark 2 : 3 - 4

{ GNT }

(3) " When four men arrived, carrying a paralyzed man to Jesus.

(4) Because of the crowd, however, they could not get the man to him. So they made a hole in the roof right above the place where Jesus was. When they had made an opening, they let the man down, lying on his mat."

Mark 2 : 3 - 4

{ ESV }

(3) " And they came, bringing to him a paralytic carried by four men.

(4) And when they could not get near him because of the crowd, they removed the roof above him, and when they had made an opening, they let down the bed on which the paralytic lay."

Mark 2 : 3 - 4

{ Heb - Gk Study Bible NIV }

(3) " Some men came, bringing to him a paralytic, carried by four of them.

(4) Since they could not get him to Jesus because of the crowd, they made an opening in the roof above Jesus, and, after digging through it, lowered the mat the paralyzed man was lying on."

The interesting thing to me in verse three and it has been there throughout the whole passage is the non - descriptive way that Mark describes the people other than Jesus Christ in the scenes he is presenting us with? The reality is that we are not given the names of the people involved, some of the crowd, whose home the meeting was being held in, the four men who brought the paralytic or even the name of the paralytic himself? My belief is that this was done deliberately by Mark, he wanted the focus to be on Jesus Christ and His actions in the situation that he was describing in this part of his gospel? If Mark had named people, the focus would be on those people, rather than on the actions of Jesus Christ in the situation? We probably would be remembering them rather than Jesus Christ. Also, the no - names , and bare bones description adds to the drama and immediacy of the drama of the situation that Mark is outlining in this section of his gospel?

Note also, that it took four men to lift the bed or mat of the paralytic man? Who were these men, what was their connection to the paralytic man? As we will see later on the four men are rather important to the story of these verses in the gospel of Mark?

What the four men did to get the paralytic man to Jesus Christ is amazing, it shows a determination to get the man unheard of? The men would do anything to get the man to Jesus Christ. Houses in that time had flat roof's and so they get on the roof and start digging into it to get the man to Jesus Christ. The roof was probably made up of earth or clay and so they would have been able to dig it up easily? Thereby making an opening to lower the bed of the paralytic man down to Jesus Christ?

The interesting thing to note , is that, the paralytic man was brought to Jesus Christ? In many instances in the gospel accounts it was Jesus Christ who sought people out to bring healing to their lives. Here we have the paralytic man being brought to Him. Through the paralytic man being brought to Jesus Christ there is a sense of expectation that permeates the gospel account of Mark at this point in it. The man has now been lowered on his bed or mat to Jesus Christ in the middle of the house Jesus is preaching in ? What will Jesus Christ do with the man now? The drama of the situation is building and building, the suspense of it is profound, we wonder what will happen to the man now?

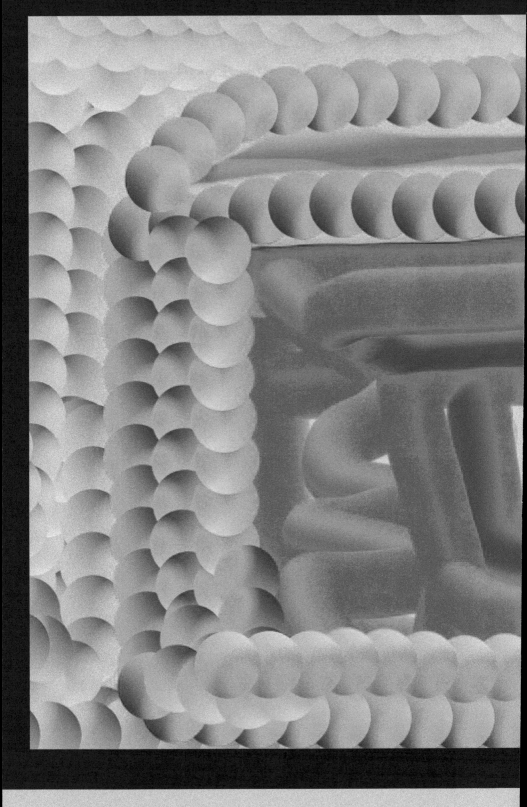

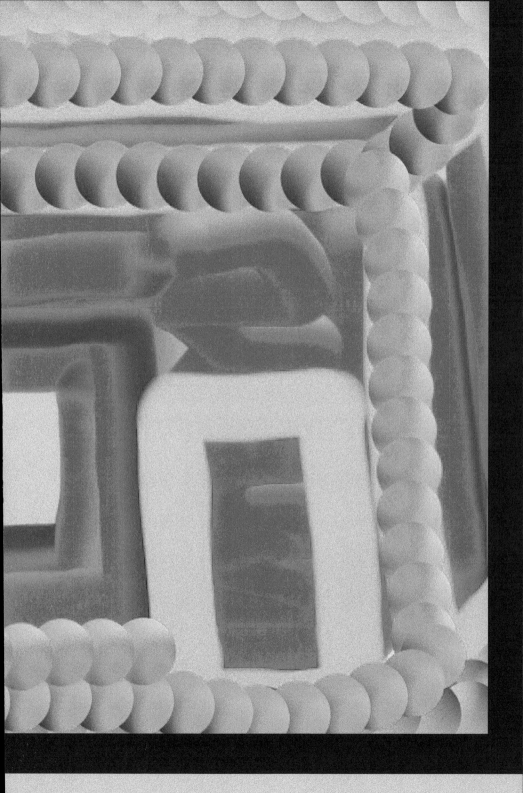

3. Verses Five and Six : - Jesus Christ ' saw the faith of the four men'.

Mark 2 : 5 - 6

{ CEB }

(5) " When Jesus saw their faith, he said to the paralytic, " Child, your sins are forgiven! "

(6)   Some legal experts, were sitting there, muttering among themselves, "

Mark 2 : 5 - 6

{ GNT}

(5) " Seeing how much faith they had, Jesus said to the paralyzed man " My son, your sins are forgiven."

(6) Some teachers of the Law who were sitting there thought to themselves."

Mark 2 : 5 - 6

{ ESV}

(5) " And when Jesus saw their faith, he said to the paralytic, ' Son, your sins are forgiven.'

(6) Now some of the scribes were sitting there, questioning in their hearts."

Mark 2 : 5 - 6

{ Heb - GK Study Bible NIV }

(5) " When Jesus saw their faith, he said to the paralytic, " Son, your sins are forgiven."

(6) Now some teachers of the law were sitting there, thinking to themselves."

For myself, verse five is one of

most important verses in Mark 2 : 1 - 12, in that, ' Jesus saw their faith.'Its interesting that Jesus does not do anything regards the paralytic man until this point of ' seeing their faith'. He probably watched them lower the paralytic man from the roof and wondered what was going on? From their actions the four men show belief, trust and even faith in Jesus Christ's ability to heal the paralytic man they have just lowered down to Him from the roof? In many ways the whole lowering of the man from the roof, seems to me to be the four men putting their faith, bellied in Jesus Christ's ability to heal the paralytic man into concrete action? The four men had probably heard of Jesus Christ's ability to heal the sick and now they wanted to believe that He could in reality heal the paralytic man they were lowering to him from the roof? They believed that Jesus Christ could work the miracle of the healing of the paralytic man, he could be made well, he could walk again?

Sometimes I do wonder what the phrase ' he saw their faith ' means? I would like to believe that Jesus Christ saw their hearts as well as their faith in action? Given, what happens later in the story of Mark 2 : 1 - 12 ; I believe Jesus Christ could well have seen through everything and seen the heart - attitude of the four men and understood that they were in fact genuine in their faith and belief?

Also, in verse five its interesting that Jesus Christ says, ' My son, your sins are forgiven.' It is not the physical healing that Jesus Christ deals with in the first instance? The man's sins being forgiven was of major importance to Jesus, the man being right with the Father positionally in terms of his sins was of first importance to Jesus Christ? So often we can overlook or underestimate the forgiveness of people's sins and major instead on their physical healing? Both are important and in Mark 2 : 1 - 12 Jesus Christ does both the forgiving of the man's sins and the physical healing of his broken body?

Verse six and the teachers of the Law or the scribes, they were watching all of this unfold before their own eyes and they were not too happy about it at all? Mark heightens the drama and tension regards the teachers of the Law , the scribes in that they mutter and think to themselves but do not speak a word against Jesus Christ and what He is doing? All of which becomes increasingly important later on in the story of the man who was healed, the paralytic man lowered through the roof to Jesus Christ?

One can imagine the scene in one's mind, the religious teacher's muttering away to themselves and spoiling for a fight with this new upstart of a religious teacher or Rabbi in Jesus Christ? He is overturning all the tables of their religious orthodoxy and orthodox religious belief regards the how things should be done and how things such as the Law should be applied practically? What will they do later on in the story of Mark 2 : 1 – 12 ?

4 . Verses Seven and Eight - the religious teachers of the Law, the scribes who were unmasked by Jesus Christ.

Mark 2 : 7 - 8

{ CEB }

(7) " Why does he speak this way? He's insulting God. Only the one God can forgive sins."

(8) Jesus immediately recognized what they were discussing, and he said to them, " Why do you fill your minds with these questions?"

Mark 2 : 7 - 8

{ Heb - GK Study Bible NIV}

(7) " Why does this fellow talk like that?

He's blaspheming ! Who can forgive sins but God alone?"

(8) Immediately Jesus knew in his spirit that this was what they were thinking in their hearts and he said to them, " Why are you thinking these things?"

Mark 2 : 7 - 8

{ ESV }

(7) " Why does this man speak like that ? He is blaspheming! Who can forgive sins but God alone?"

(8) And immediately Jesus, perceiving in his spirit that they thus questioned within themselves, said to them, " Why do you question these things in your hearts?"

Mark 2 : 7 - 8

{ GNT}

(7) " How does he dare talk like this? This is blasphemy! God is the only one who can forgive sins!"

(8) At once Jesus knew what they were thinking , so he said to them, " Why do you think such things?"

Verse Seven gives us the reader an insight into the self - talk of the religious teachers of the Law and the scribes. They do not like what Jesus Christ is saying and doing in this house in Caperrnaum? After all they were the religious teachers of the Law, they were the ones who had been trained to interpret and apply to life situations to the Law, who was He? Their self - talk betrays their heart motivation and they are sitting there in the mistaken belief that nobody knows what they are thinking?

Yet, in verse eight there is an

immediacy to Jesus Christ perceiving and coming to understand and see what they are thinking and have been muttering to themselves about? Jesus Christ would have known who these men were, the esteemed scribes and teachers of the Law come to check up on Him? They probably came all the way from Jerusalem to do it as well?

To me this is the other miracle that takes place in Mark 2 : 1 - 12; its not just the miracle of the physical healing of the paralytic on show but also there is the miracle of the spiritual perception of Jesus Christ on show as well? Jesus Christ was able to immediately perceive and understand and even read what they were thinking to themselves in their minds without them vocalizing a word? I do not know about you but to me that is indeed a miracle on the part of Jesus Christ?

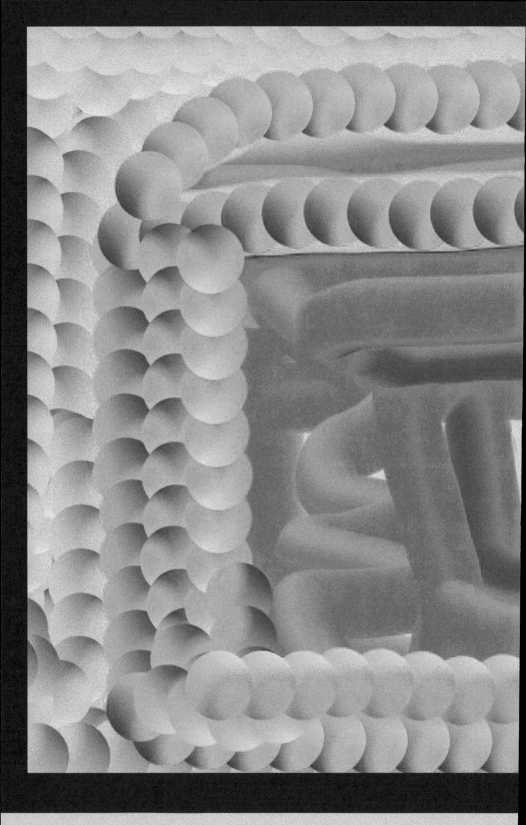

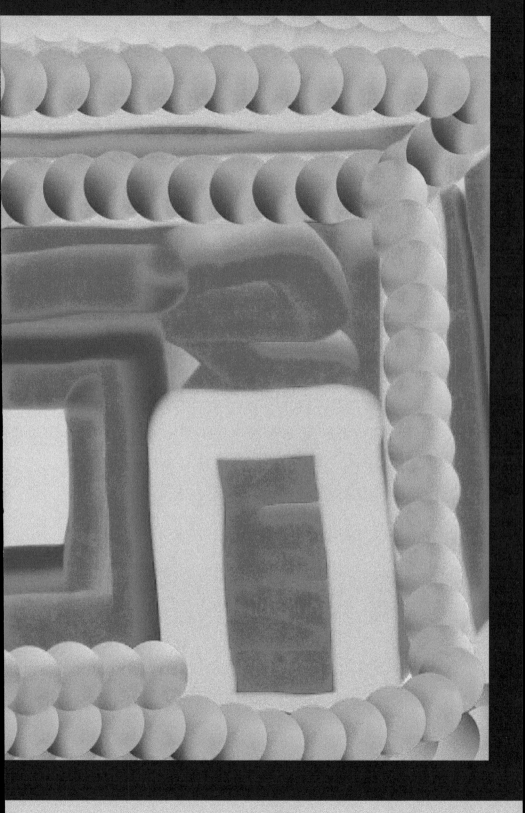

5 . Verses Nine and Ten.

Mark 2 : 9 - 10

{CEB}

(9) " Which is easier - to say to a paralyzed person, ' Your sins are forgiven', or to say, ' Get up, take up your bed, and walk?'

(10) But so you will know that the Human One has authority on the earth to forgive sins" - he said to the man who was paralyzed"

Mark 2 : 9 - 10

{ Heb - GK Study Bible NIV }

(9) " Which is easier : to say to the paralytic, ' Your sins are forgiven,' or to say, ' Get up, take up your mat and walk?"

(10) But that you may know that the Son of Man has authority on earth to forgive sins ....."He said to the paralytic, "

Mark 2 : 9 - 10

{ ESV }

(9) " Which is easier, to say to the paralytic, ' Your sins are forgiven', or to say, ' Rise, take up your bed and walk?'

(10) But that you may know that the Son of Man has authority on earth to forgive sins" - he said to the paralytic - "

Mark 2 : 9 - 10

{GNT}

(9) " Is it easier to say to this paralyzed man,
' Your sins are forgiven,' or to say, ' Get up,

pick up your mat, and walk?'

(10) I will prove to you, then, that the Son of Man has authority on earth to forgive sins." So he said to the paralyzed man."

In verse nine Jesus Christ turns the questioning back onto the religious teachers and scribes and asks them a probing question He wants them attempt to answer for Him? Its like the ultimate hypothetical question or scenario Jesus Christ pulls out of the air to pose to the religious teachers and scribes, ' Yous say this, I say this '. What is right in your eyes to do, forgive sins, or to heal the paralytic man of paralysis? Its almost like Jesus Christ is playing the ultimate form of ' Truth and Dare' with the religious teachers and scribes? He has already showed them that He knows and understands their thinking and ways of operating to the ultimate degree?

The question Jesus Christ poses, hangs in the air, will the religious teachers and scribes answer the question He has posed to them? What will be their response be to His question?

The ' but ' in verse ten is very significant He takes the right of response to His own probing question and scenario of verse nine out of the religious teachers and scribes hands? He has something He really thinks the religious teachers and scribes really need to know and come to understanding of ; as to what is really happening in the house in Caperrnaum on the night they are present in the house?

Again, it is the authority question, they have questioned His authority to forgive sins? They realist full well and understand that in doing that he is equating Himself with God, the Son of God? Yet its interesting that Jesus uses the term Son of Man to refer to Himself ?

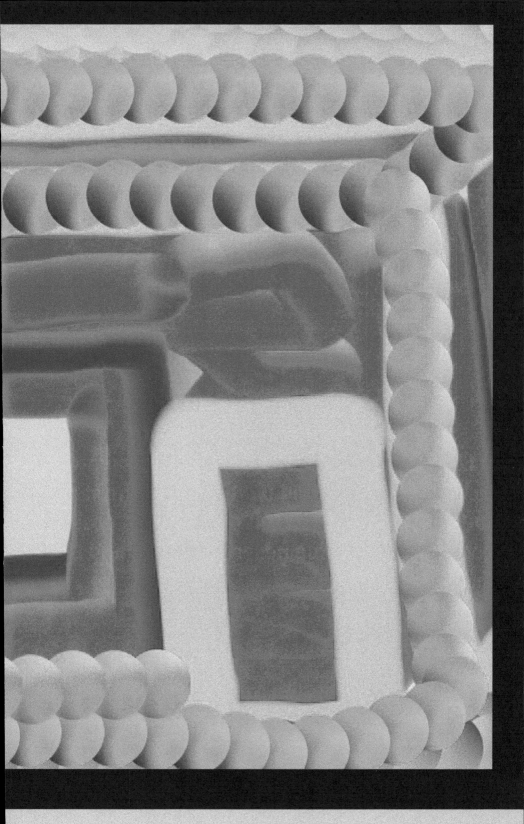

6 . Verses Eleven and Twelve - the end of the story of the man who was healed or is it rather the beginning of our story with Jesus Christ in terms of Him healing our own brokenness and pain in our own lives?

Mark 2 : 11 - 12

{ CEB }

(11) " Get up, take your mat, and go home."

(12) " Jesus raised him up, and right away he picked up his mat and walked out in front of everybody, They were all amazed and praised God, saying, " We've never seen anything like this!"

Mark 2 : 11 - 12

{ Heb - Gk Study Bible NIV }

(11) " I tell you, get up, take your mat and go home."

(12) " He got up, took his mat and walked out in full view of them all. This amazed everyone and they praised God, saying, " We have never seen anything like this!"

Mark 2 : 11 - 12

{ ESV }

(11) " I say to you, rise, pick up your bed, and go home."

(12) " And he rose and immediately picked up his bed and went out before them all, so that they were all amazed and glorified God, saying," We never saw anything like this!"

Mark 2 : 11 - 12

{ GNT }

(11) " I tell you, get up, pick up your mat, and go home !"

(12) " While they all watched, the man got up, picked up his mat, and hurried away. They were all completely amazed and praised God, saying, " We have never seen anything like this!"

This is the final two verses of Mark 2 : 11 - 12, and what verses they are, profound and moving at the same time? The drama of the proceeding verses has now reached its crescendo, the man has now finally been healed by God and set free from his paralysis?

The words ' get up ' can mean to wake up, or to raise up, which i find interesting to note and understand? Jesus

Christ commands the paralytic to raise up, come back to life and wholeness of mind, body and spirit? There has been much more than just the physical healing of the paralytic man on show in these verses , for both the man himself , for the audience present in the house in Caperrnaum and even for us as the later readers of this story in Mark's gospel?

Jesus Christ in verse 11 and 12 eloquently puts His credit-ails as the Son of Man on display for all to see. He can both forgive sins and also bring physical healing to the broken body of the paralytic man? He reveals both the power and authority that he carries as the Son of Man, Son of God, the Messiah. Power and authority from God the Father Himself? Even the religious teachers and scribes are amazed and dumbfounded when the paralytic man gets to his feet and takes up his mat and goes back to his home?

In many ways Jesus Christ's display of His authority to both forgive sins and heal people's bodies silences the critics in the form of the religious teachers and scribes. They now have no further comeback , there is nothing more they can say to Jesus Christ or even require of Him? The actions of Jesus Christ as the Son of Man have answered all the questions that have been hanging in the air since the story of the paralytic started in Mark 2?

Its also interesting that everyone in the room praises God, they attribute what they have just seen in the form of the healing of the paralytic man to God Himself? Thereby it answers to some degree early on in Mark's gospel the question and questions people had as to who Jesus Christ was? The divinity question and the authority question have been answered and yet they will remain central questions about Jesus Christ in the gospel of Mark?

Finally, the last statement ' we have never seen anything like this '; testifies to the reality of Jesus Christ bringing with Himself a whole new way of doing things, and responding to the suffering and pain of people. As well the sinfulness of people and the weight and burden they carried regards it? The Kingdom of God had come in the form of the life and ministry of Jesus Christ. He was and still is ' Emmanuel ' ; God with us?

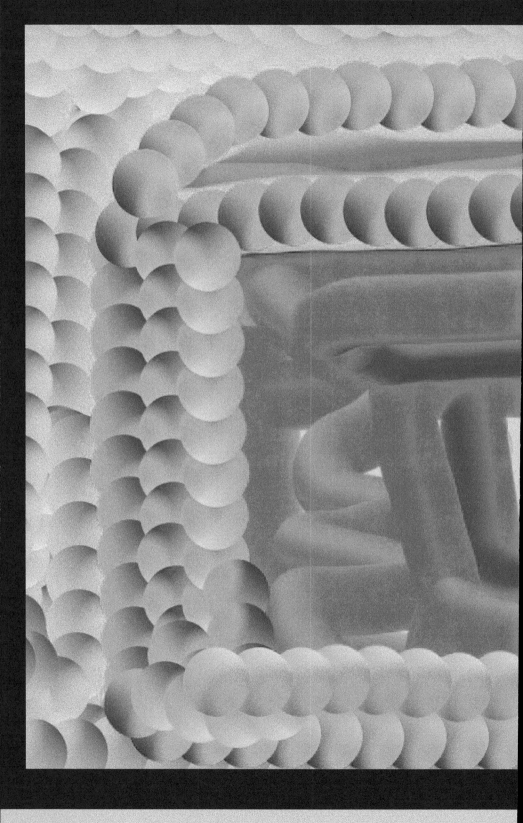

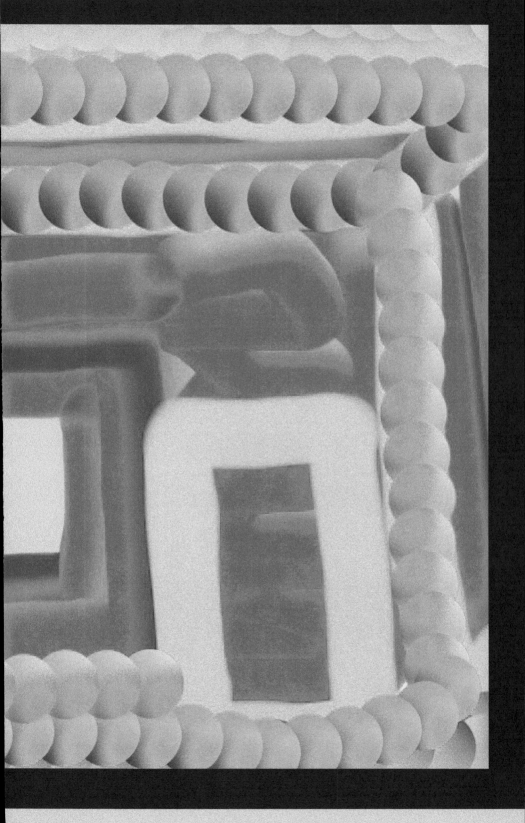

EPILOGUE :

The Healing of A Man, has sought to deal with the story of the healing of the paralytic man in Mark 2 : 1 - 12. It has been seen that there is so much more to this couple of verses in the gospel of Mark than just the physical healing of the paralytic man? In the end it is a question of who Jesus Christ was and is, where His power and authority came from?

Also, whether or not He really is the Son of Man, as seen in the book of Daniel, who has now come to earth and the people of God Israel? The question is what will people do with Him once they come to understand and see who He is?

We saw the faith and belief of the four men on display in the story of the paralytic man, and even how it was both used and honored by Jesus Christ Himself?

Its a drama packed, edge of your seat thriller of a story, it keeps you engaged with it to its conclusion, the physical healing of the paralytic man? The Son of Man has displayed His power and authority for all to see and to come to an understanding of it for themselves?

Amen, amen and
amen .

Shalom!